I0435880

Eagles
Soar On High Thermals

Terence George Craddock

BALBOA
PRESS
A DIVISION OF HAY HOUSE

Copyright © 2016 Terence George Craddock.

All rights reserved. No part of this book may be used or reproduced
by any means, graphic, electronic, or mechanical, including
photocopying, recording, taping or by any information storage retrieval
system without the written permission of the author except in the
case of brief quotations embodied in critical articles and reviews.

Balboa Press books may be ordered through booksellers or by contacting:

Balboa Press
A Division of Hay House
1663 Liberty Drive
Bloomington, IN 47403
www.balboapress.com.au
1 (877) 407-4847

Because of the dynamic nature of the Internet, any web addresses or
links contained in this book may have changed since publication and
may no longer be valid. The views expressed in this work are solely those
of the author and do not necessarily reflect the views of the publisher,
and the publisher hereby disclaims any responsibility for them.

The author of this book does not dispense medical advice or prescribe
the use of any technique as a form of treatment for physical, emotional,
or medical problems without the advice of a physician, either directly
or indirectly. The intent of the author is only to offer information
of a general nature to help you in your quest for emotional and
spiritual well-being. In the event you use any of the information in
this book for yourself, which is your constitutional right, the author
and the publisher assume no responsibility for your actions.

Any people depicted in stock imagery provided by Thinkstock are
models, and such images are being used for illustrative purposes only.
Certain stock imagery © Thinkstock.

Print information available on the last page.

ISBN: 978-1-5043-0452-8 (sc)
ISBN: 978-1-5043-0453-5 (e)

Balboa Press rev. date: 10/17/2016

Craddock has taken themes of nature, time, cosmic consciousness, mysticism, transcendentalism, personalism, which Walt Whitman explored in his esteemed volume of poetry *Leaves of Grass*, and pursued their meaning with contemporary scientific discoverys. There are tides in nature and tides in human societies, countries and civilizations, which embrace interact or reject changing perspectives of nature.

Eagles Soar On High Thermals highlights explores individual and social awareness sown into contemporary and past perceptions of life and nature. The reader will embark upon a facinating refreshing journey into nature, encompassed within the cosmic galactic to the microscopic, ecosystems of life from natural landscapes, to human interactive sentiment viewpoints lifestyles, merging into mystic perceptions.

Nature is radiant infused with a spiritual sacredness, blessings of life, in the vibrant prestine wilderness of untamed lands, diversity profound landscapes interact in ecosystems dissimilar and each unique environment blessing bestows beauty; upon all eyes stopping to view perceive contemplate an operatic ballet of life endlessly displayed in nature.

A must read for inquisitive minds desiring to pursue poetic expression, thoughts engaging with insights into enduring mysteries of life and nature. Embedded within the text is a wonderful diversity, a spiritual harmonic love appreciation of nature, from cosmic creation to various forms of human interaction with our planet's environments, which we must choose to preserve and cherish or continue to abuse at our own peril.

This volume of verse is dedicated to all people who love

appreciate and enjoy the exquisite beauty of awesome nature,

especially to those who strieve to preserve the wilderness

and the pristine diversity of protected natural ecosystems.

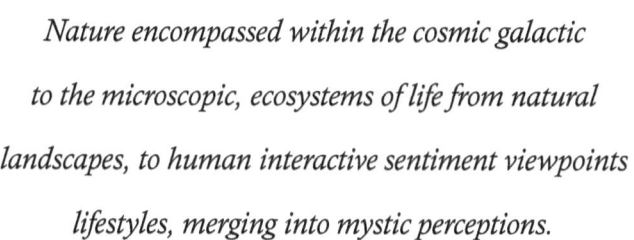

Nature encompassed within the cosmic galactic
to the microscopic, ecosystems of life from natural
landscapes, to human interactive sentiment viewpoints
lifestyles, merging into mystic perceptions.

Contents

Alphabetical Order

Let The Butterfly Fly Free
Life As Surface Realities
Life Feasts Still Feed Old Hunters
Life Principle
Life Time Transformations
Life Tossed By Waves In A Storm
Liquid Concussion
Liquid Pigment
Liquid Screams Smoke Dance
Liquid Screams Thunder Air Dance
Love Cast In Spotlight Eternity
Metamorphosis
Out Gunned By A Single Cell DNA Rocker
Pebble Passage Through Water
Photosynthesis Earth Sphere
Picasso Minds
Poetic Waters
Pollen Call Is Rainbow Pot Of Gold To El Dorado
Rain Fall Pantomime
Ravished Vein
Rhine Wine
Sacred Life Honoured
Serenade Under A Blood Red Yellow Moon
She Awaits A Moonlit Serenade
Ships Passing In Night Born
Silence
Snow And Rain
Stardust Seeds Dream Life
'Still I Rise' by Maya Angelou Do You?
Stir Like Flashes Of Moonlight
Summit Mt Everest Death Zone Tested
Sun Seeking Flies
The Common Sea Of Humanity
The Gift Of Art
The Impossibility Of Identical Snowflakes

Titles By Date

Erosion II Written in June 1994.
To A Cat Written in April 1995 on the 18.4.1995.
Silence Written in April 1995 on the 21.4.1995.
Warm Milk At Bedtime Written in
    May 1995 on the 11.5.1995.
Ebb Tide Written in October 1996 on the 21.10.1996.
Earth Chill Written in March 1998 on the 3.3.1998.
Liquid Pigment Written in March 1998 on the 3.3.1998.
Ravished Vein Written in March 1998 on the 3.3.1998.
Fly Buzzing Naked Skin Written in
    May 1998 on the 2&3.5.98. 3
Sun Seeking Flies Written in May
    1998 on the 2&3.5.98. 6
Dog Soldier Lodge Affirmed Written
    in July 1998 on the 25.7.1998.
Thought Waves Written in July 1998 on the 25.7.1998.
Feathered Connection Written in May
    1999 on the 18.5.1999.
The Common Sea Of Humanity Written
    in May 1999 on the 19.5.1999.
Life Principle Written in October 1999 on the 4.10.1999.
Eagles Soar On High Thermals Written in
    November 1999 on the 12.11.1999. 1
Eagle Eyries Written in November
    1999 on the 12.11.1999. 2
Eagle Flight Written in November
    1999 on the 12.11.1999. 3
Eagle Sight Written in November
    1999 on the 12.11.1999. 4
Eagle Spirit Written in November
    1999 on the 12.11.1999. 5

Stir Like Flashes Of Moonlight Written in
February 2010 on the 13.2.2010.
Children Of Dust Written in February
2010 on the 16.2.2010.
Cultural Heritage Nurtured Written in
February 2010 on the 16.2.2010.
Transformation Peril Written in February
2010 on the 16.2.2010.
A Stone Griffin Written in March 2010 on the 3.2010.
Drink Me Eat Me Written in March
2010 on the 19&25.3.2010.
China Moon Written in April 2010 on the 2.4.2010.
Ego Of Immense Proportions Written in
April 2010 on the 11.4.2010.
Rhine Wine Written in April 2010 on the 12.4.2010.
A Heritage Of Aussie Drought Written in January
& April 2010 on the 27.1&16.4.2010.
Great Beauty Past And Present Written
in May 2010 on the 1.5.2010.
A Second Sight Written in May 2010 on the 11.5.2010.
Hand Of The Infinite Written in June
2010 on the 4.6.2010.
Darkness Split Second Broken Written
in June 2010 on the 10.6.2010.
The Pelican Brief Written in June
2010 on the 25.6.2010.
A River Dies Written in July 2010 on the 4.7.2010.
Into The Looking Glass Written in
July 2010 on the 25.7.2010.
Diamond Mine Written in July 2010 on the 31.7.2010.
'Still I Rise' by Maya Angelou Do You? Written
in August 2010 on the 15.8.2010.
Freedom Drum Beats Within Storm Front
Written in August 2010 on the 17.8.2010.

A View Through Depths Of Creation Written
in August 2010 on the 18.8.2010.
High School Science Project Written in
August 2010 on the 22.8.2010.
Hidden Valley Within The Bush Written in
August 2010 on the 26.8.2010. 5
Ghost Towns Up On The Hill Written in
August 2010 on the 26.8.2010. 6
Life Feasts Still Feed Old Hunters Written
in August 2010 on the 26.8.2010. 7
Fruit Not Felled By The Wind Written in
August 2010 on the 26.8.2010. 8
Angels Harmonic Serenade Written in
August 2010 on the 28.8.2010. 2
Cats Are Written in August 2010 on the 28.8.2010. 6
Visions In Sweat Lodge Written in
August 2010 on the 29.8.2010.
An Indian Summer Written in August
2010 on the 30.8.2010.
Picasso Minds Written in September
2010 on the 2.9.2010.
Serenade Under A Blood Red Yellow Moon Written
in September 2010 on the 19.9.2010. 2
Beauty Is Found Written in September
2010 on the 19.9.2010. 3
In Leaf Fall Learn Written in September
2010 on the 23.9.2010.
An Eternal Summer Written in September
2010 on the 24.9.2010.
Earth Pulse Written in October 2010 on the 6.10.2010.
Fire In The Sky Written in October
2010 on the 8.10.2010.
Poetic Waters Written in October
2010 on the 9.10.2010. 1

Erosion II

Trees are teardrops
secreted upon porcelain cliffs
asparagus stems severed
cut clipped stumps
greedily gobbled globules
of virile all mother

sacrificed shaft shorn
as arid chalk
fractures
beneath rooted veins
veldt
fallows featureless

winds whip
weeping welts
rains weave
woe wilful
dust devils
dance delighted

over desert
deserted environs
earth mother
ebbs eradicated
sacrifices subdues
rabid man beast

. . . momentarily

Written in June 1994.

High School Science Project

in the celestrial
scheme of things
this world
planet earth

this sacred world
earth sphere planet
ball blue life bubble
spin life day night

if it were rated
a high school
science project
how judge you?

conception creation potential
planet water land masses
flora plants fauna animals
micro systems eco systems

life domain kingdom
phylum/division
class order family
genus species outlined

an animal kingdom
split into main groups
vertebrates (with a backbone)
invertebrates (without a backbone)

an animal a mouse a cat
a dog or a lion or tiger
over 800,000 species
have now been identified

in the Animal Kingdom
most species are in
the Arthropod phylum
mind blowing numbers

scientists estimate
to identify all species
in the tropical rain
forests the ranks of

Arthropoda would swell
to over 10 million species!
A clam a jellyfish an insect
an earthworm all are animal.

How rate you now
this celestrial high
school science project?
Can any judge detect

a cosmic finger of God
any data evidence of
intelligent DNA design?
Or random evolution?

Written in August 2010 on the 22.8.2010.
Phylum Arthropoda, the largest animal phyla,
now has over 1 million species identified.

An Amoebia Of
Transformative Thought

consider single
cell amoebia
of plied ego
essential character
amazing still
largest sequenced
genome known
still rocking

at the top
of base pairs
genome DNA
charts
bothering
no one
busy
about business

early earth
conquered
primal soup
Amoebia Dubia
genome size
DNA champion
rock on tease
mysterious

mystery
single-celled
organism
lodging
in water
in moist soil
on land
or invasive

as a parasite
of communion
host organisms
protoplasmic
mass in thin
membrane
free of fixed
cage form

supporting
structures
transmute
temporary
projections
pseudopodia
locomotion
to journey

Written in December 2010 on the 29.12.2010.

Silence

There is silence.
When the birds stop singing.
And the world waits.

Then The Great Spirit
may speak when we listen.
To the wisdom of silence.

Written in April 1995 on the 21.4.1995.

Visions In Sweat Lodge

could not carry fast burden painting
soul quickened in joy heart stirring
soul porous fevers in clay ash sweat
time runs ahead images lack context
drown in dream visions guide swirling

Written in August 2010 on the 29.8.2010.

Thunderbird Spirit Flight

so often repeating
same patterns
ingrained behaviour

behaviour man tribe choice

touch me not
thoughts thunder
I breathe not

thunder lightning storms
wake all senses rebirth mind
in storms elemental life

I breathe sound whips
see light rays ionize retina
storms infuse life pores

flight wings beat
thunder claps in day night sky
mouth eyes open

close mouth
creation words
cause lightbolts

witness universe
echo creation dance
boy sky eyes sees

speaks backwards writes
signs ritual wind stirs clouds script
light bred shades sky signs

eagle eyes hurricane flashes
flies thunderbird dimensions sight
darting vision sight wisdom's

intelligent powerful wrathful
worm greed tribe man breeds material
earth rape stirs thunderbird

anger in sacred mountains vast
Great Spirit sends thunderbird spirit
messages to spirit who listens

listen child tree of life
holds nest creation within
life branches sundance

while sun still shines
raise arms reach hands
embrace life visions

Written in November 2010 on 1.11.2010.

Dog Soldier Lodge Affirmed

We believed in love, freedom, nobility;
    to spiritual depths of our souls.
We believed in spiritual sacredness;
    of our vibrant untamed land.
We rode our mustangs like wind tossed rolling thunder;
    drumming across within prairie storm front;
as we rode wild free ranging prairie wind;
    sweeping across an untamed unshod land.

We were so proud to live; as robust hunter-warriors;
    to walk stand tall; sharing tribal life spirit.
So proud to live! So proud to die!

We fought frightened forked tongued white devil;
    with every honourable fibre of our sacred being;
as they swept like vermin; despoiling stealing violating;
    great beauty of a spiritual primeval land.
As Dog Soldier Warriors; of entrusted sacred lodge;
    we died as we lived; with respect spiritual nobility.
I remember drums beating beating beating . . . .
    as my tribe cast my sacred spirit free.

I remember ritual tribal drums beating;
    as my people cast my shaman spirit free;
vanquishing suppressed pain of weeping wounds;
    which had battle pierced bled profusely;
sustained in mesmeric dance of necessitated battle;
    when trampled buffalo hide tepee;
    of venerated Great Spirit;
    within my warrior hardened body;
    invincible in combat;
    finally fell undefeated; before an ignoble enemy.

Defend ancestral hunting grounds;
wearer of eagle feathered;
    war bonnet; strike with medicine
    power; of eagle descending . . . .
on prey; protect shaman warrior;
brave deeds in battle worthy;
    first to touch living fallen enemy in
    battle; in front of fighting . . . .
notched decorated feathers tell your
deeds; designate swift killing;
    telling your fierce individual stories;
    scalping capturing . . . .
enemy's weapons shield proudly worn;
how thunder on horseback
    or foot; attacking fear you struck into
    veteran civil war enemies . . . .

What remained of a once proud
people; hostilities long bled;
    cast my shaman spirit free; cleansing
    ceremony completing;
to roam restoring; releasing vitality;
warrior leading retaliatory strikes;
    be free in spiritual hunting ground;
    of earned nomadic nobility.
Until foretold time; descendant tribe;
would seek; must seek;
    wisdom of spirit world; to guide
    survivors in spiritual perpetuity.

Then search in sacred ritual circle
ceremony; tribal knowledge proving;
    for tribal lore; for primeval knowledge;
    for new found spirituality.

Guarded for time swept tribe; for time of great need;
    by a shaman; by a newborn past
    ancestor; of awe inspiring ability.
We worshipped; in peace in war;
wisdom of Great Spirit.
    We worshipped life. We worshipped
    our land. In perpetuity.

Written in July 1998 on the 24.7.1998.

Blessings Of Life

rain good friend to soil
your blessing is soft moist earth
rain good friend to plants
your blessing is fruitful growing life

rain good friend to animals
your blessing is healthy vibrant diversity
rain good friend to dry land
your blessing is lakes streams rivers

rain everywhere I rapture look
yours blessing bestows beauty

Written in October 2010 on the 24.10.2010.

Fire In The Sky

heat light sunlight
particle wave energy
radiant solar wind

heat light sunlight
flowing from globe sun
these critical parts

fuel for an ecosystem

sun's gift heat
helps water evaporate
return to atmosphere

evaporate purify
cycled back
into purer water

sun's gift heat
helps keep plants
helps keep animals
blanket warm

without light
light gift from sun
there cannot be

there is no
photosynthesis
plants destitute

would not
have energy
needed

to make food
volcanic vents
on ocean floor

supply energy
but not scale
photosynthesis

fire in the sky
supplies oceans
life energy

photosynthesis
at sea on land
is ocean gift life

science creation in harmony
nature's laws are God's laws
interlocking interrelated laws

harmony is balance in creation

are we not all parts of creation?

Written in October 2010 on the 8.10.2010.

Pebble Passage Through Water

pebble rough pebble
smooth seen
vein colour adored

which makes
most beautiful ripples
on dark water?

behold beauty
of ripples
forget not
sound of entry

Written in October 2010 on the 9.10.2010.

Poetic Waters

behold this vast lake
silent serene waters
moonlight shimmers
upon life ephemeral
crystal cut wavelets

crystal wavelets dance
whisper in moonlit breeze
breeze blow cool upon
warm flesh homage perceiving
perceiving wisdom in vast

depth shimmer creative waters

in dawn's yellow finger
light fresh beauty focus shapes
depth colour light touch
sound scent stir movement
life springs forth creates

creation dawn serenade
smell scent rhythm fresh
before hot overhead noon sun
time bestows eyes philosophy
divinity mind dream wakes

cast a pebble
upon surface
light reflective waters
watch time
spread wave rings

spread forth uniform
wave ripples spread forth
harmonic embrace minds

pebble sinks
deep embrace
welcomed by
wisdom's waters
pebble rough

or smooth
passed on
seen in
third eye
memory

pebble or rock
shaped perception
is ever gone
seen no more
passage enfolds

enlightenment

shape formatic embraces
review rapid ripples harmonic
contemplate message symmetry
singer sing songs freeborn
on breeze string stir vibrations

remember
wisdom encoded
words
singer rock
are seen no more

Written in October 2010 on the 9.10.2010.

Picasso Minds

free range minds must ride
wild vast emotive prairie winds

immerse into deep depths
explore huge diverse oceans

fools put limitation frames upon
quantum childhood imaginations

Written in September 2010 on the 2.9.2010.

Rain Fall Pantomime

rain down pour sudden
surge sheets tropical
smoke scorched roof titles

Written in December 2010 on the 26.12.2010.

Liquid Concussion

sound reverberates circulates soars
liquid concussion echo ground beats
water slip streams far reach impacts

Written in December 2010 on the 26.12.2010.

Liquid Screams Smoke Dance

mist swirls wind dance
smoke steam instant evaporation
bow libations rain dance

Written in December 2010 on the 26.12.2010.

Liquid Screams
Thunder Air Dance

rain down pour sudden
surge sheets tropical
smoke scorched roof titles

mist swirls wind dance
smoke steam instant evaporation
bow libations rain dance

sound reverberates circulates soars
liquid concussion echo ground beats
water slip streams far reach impacts

Written in December 2010 on the 26.12.2010.

Experience Cosmic Whisper

experience
mind
non-talkative

experience
past
present future

experience
time
as eternity

split
second
causality

single
moment
eternity

cosmic
whisper
eureka

Written in October 2010 on the 11.10.2010.

To A Cat

The big fat cat
is sitting on the mat.
Sitting by the fire
no feline time for hire.

No cares today
no master in any way.
In a warm well lit room
every comfort always groomed.

Do not spin or sow
no difficult path to hoe.
So evolved will not try
so will never peach verdant sky.

Written in April 1995 on the 18.4.1995.

Warm Milk At Bedtime

Coy covetous cat
snuggled up in bed
secure
in warmth love.

Darkness
a goose-down quilt
cover
her slender form.

Youngest son
on left
husband
eldest son
on right.

You can almost
hear her purring.
She can drink
this kind
of milk forever.

Written in May 1995 on the 11.5.1995.

Cats Are

cats are
they come go
accept reject

in independent thought
in secret feline thought
loyal to moments in time

enjoying totally in luxury
exultation of comfort purring
day vision night vision shifts

shifting in time
shifting in mind
shifting in mood

light changes seen through
optical shifts in feline slit eyes
adjusting light sound perception

living moments lapping contentment
changes changes of timeless sleep

Written in August 2010 on the 28.8.2010.

Freedom Drum Beats
Within Storm Front

mustangs race wind tossed rolling thunder
hoof beats drum prairie storm front
freedom races wild free ranging prairie wind

Written in August 2010 on the 17.8.2010.

Ebb Tide

it is late now
very late dusk's
darkness has
already fallen

dark rimmed sunset
disappear last glow
dissipate be gone
fade away

this night is silk warm
flesh is sun kiss warm
breeze soft caress warm

waves wash out
footprints softly splash
suck in sink sand

feet grow cool
sunken treasure sands
slowly shape mould

harmonic planes
miniature waves wisps
whisper gliding in
shallows on seabreeze

washing out ripples
migrating miniature waves
single summer's seascape

sifting sands
blown skip briskly
sting the windward
inward spirit eye

the night is warm
flesh is warm
breeze is warm
soul is warm

Written in October 1996 on the 21.10.1996.

Life Tossed By Waves
In A Storm

Life stasis is a calm wave
swept breath beach
smooth sand tide swept.
Life storms preach
motion change dynamic fluid.

Lizzie Limpet should
have rocked on
exploration has benefits.
Clinging to a rock
is leave ever beached.

Staying clamped
in one place life caged
a stick-at-home
stuck stick in the mud
is denial lesson fixed.

Written in December 2010 on the 10.12.2010.
Lizzie Limpet is a character in a story by Edith Annie
Howes, a New Zealand teacher, visionary educationalist
and writer of approximately thirty children's books.

Ships Passing In Night Born

ships are sailing upon turn tide flowing river waters
light is dance happy mellow yellows closing long day
soon sunset will add flame reds fingers yellow gold
sun sets sinks into still sea upon horizon home shores
dust light fades shadows creep in stealth murky images
suddenly black dawns night deep
darkness speaks in glory

starlight sparkles upon enchanted
waters river ebbs flows
passage across bar out into ocean waves rocks emotions
soon short journeys made upon
ocean waters salts senses
watch shoreline beach grey sands
invisible stretch wet away
waters dark painted ocean oil black
sparkles in flow waves
beach sands perfume night with
residue heat breeze vapours

Written in October 2010 on the 17.10.2010.

Ephemeral Tide Flows
Swift In Time Darkness

watch soft silent silhouettes
surreal ships life passing otter
shapes carried slip satin water
river flows past earth shores

darkness consume illumini sunlit air
darkness consume crypt fading light
darkness paints shapes in birth night
darkness spotlight starlit atmosphere

shapes disappear dance glossomer darkness
photostream merge embue mist ink absorbing
passing ships hint images spectrums tugging
ephemeral tide flows swift in time darkness

Written in October 2010 on the 22.10.2010.

Earth Chill

Mine Black Empty
Water Dripping Chill Within
Weep Weep Raped Land.

Written in March 1998 on the 3.3.1998.

Ravished Vein

Gold Mine Echo Hollow
Ravished Vein Bled Vein
Glitter Glitter Gone.

Written in March 1998 on the 3.3.98.

Liquid Pigment

Colour Splashed Page
Liquid Pigment Washes
Raw Emotion Revealed.

Written in March 1998 on the 3.3.1998.

Thought Waves

Thought waves flow
and transmute
as they transform
across the cosmic continuum.

The beauty of the thought
transforms everything;
from the beauty
of the crystalline thought;
seasoned souls shine
forth radiantly.

Through the beauty of the thought
flows the beauty of the soul
from the beauty of the thought
from the beauty of the soul.

From flesh that was receptive
to flesh or form that was adored;
as the beauty of love grows
instinctively naturally;
thus love complimented
guides throughout eternity.

Written in July 1998 on the 25.7.98.

Feathered Connection

I understand rationalism
the paradox of the problem
interaction of integer
when in acquitted relationship.

It is hard
to fly like an eagle
when you walk
with a turkey.

At least lost luminous
forbidden false rendezvous
inserts life pain and solace
into activated bloodstream.

An eagle chick evolving must forsake
flightless earthbound existence
before it attains thermal freedom soaring
hallowed heights unchained.

Written in May 1999 on the 18.5.99.

Eagles Soar On
High Thermals

eagles soar
on high thermals
fly through
such wonderous
freeborn skies

a multiversality
kaleidoscopic
sensual

spiritual
ever changing
seasons

Written in November 1999 on the 12.11.1999.

Eagle Eyries

nest on highest
most noble
sun eclipsed
inaccessible crags
or vibrant

living temples
trees raising
towards heaven
growing upwards
into host life

giving light

Written in November 1999 on the 12.11.1999.

Eagle Flight

range soar
across desolate
canyons
holy places
where Native

Americans
built pueblo
adobe houses

care houses
upon spiritual
sun paths . . .

Written in November 1999 on the 12.11.1999.

Eagle Sight

piercingly
beautiful
sky images

celebrating
auras
earth heat

thermal
energy fields
keen eyes

pierce
heat
waves

Written in November 1999 on the 12.11.1999.

Eagle Spirit

eagles soar
on high thermals
fly through
such wonderous
freeborn skies

a multiversality
kaleidoscopic
sensual

spiritual
ever changing
seasons

nest on highest
most noble
sun eclipsed
inaccessible crags
or vibrant

living temples
trees raising
towards heaven
growing upwards
into host life

giving light

range soar
across desolate
canyons
holy places
where Native

Americans
built pueblo
adobe houses

care houses
upon spiritual
sun paths . . .

piercingly
beautiful
sky images

celebrating
auras
earth heat

thermal
energy fields
keen eyes

pierce heat
waves

Written in November 1999 on the 12.11.1999.

Summit Mt Everest
Death Zone Tested

ego skilled self-esteem
may summit Mt Everest
in heights rarified inflated . . .
feeling approach supremacy
climb into thin air past . . .

death zone 8000 metres
temperatures chill low level
frostbite extremities body parts . . .
exposed to contact ice air
snow shaded well-frozen . . .

deaths injury mistake slipping
falling stalks pounces high winds
threatens life diced changeable . . .
potential threat stalks climbers
baited breath altitude on Everest . . .

low atmospheric pressure
at summit alluring on Everest
about a third of sea level . . .
low pressure resulting in
availability in limited about . . .

a deprivation starved third oxygen
left to breathe in blood oxygen level
summit plummets expunged depleted . . .
vastly increased pace breathing rate
times three four hundred percent . . .

exhaustion attempting to breathe
lacking oxygen extreme cold
climbing hazards all contribute . . .
to death zone death toll an injured
climber who cannot walk is in . . .

serious threatening life trouble
rescue by helicopter death zone
too high cannot peak fly carrying . . .
a climber off death zone heights
reaper Everest is extremely risky . . .

only skilled egos climb Everest
battle fierce three harsh masters
consciousness mind edge memory
to reconcile claims demands weary
control planning confirming reality

unconscious psyche source deep
primitive impulses drives id fears
superego conscience morals forms
standards rules ethical choice society
summit triumph or rescue lost attempt

Written in December 2010 on the 26.12.2010.

The Impossibility Of
Identical Snowflakes

Once upon a time
throughout most of
the twentieth century

it was believed no
two snowflakes
could be exactly alike.

Mathematically it is
highly unlikely
for two snowflakes
to be exactly alike.

This is due to
the roughly
10 to power 19

water molecules
which make up
a snowflake.

Snowflakes grow
at different rates
in different patterns.

The snowflake
growth rate pattern
probabilities vary

depending on
changing temperature
changing humidity

within the atmosphere
the snowflake
growth falls through

on its journey
to the ground
gravity induced.

The dawn birth
of snowflake
scientific research

began in 1885
initial attempts
to identify find

identical twin snowflakes
by photographing
thousands of snowflakes.

Wilson Alwyn Bentley
using a microscope
found the wide variety

of classic snowflakes
forms known today
in eye matching detail.

Probability theory
holds it is more likely
that two snowflakes

could become virtually
identical if their changing
temperature humidity

environments
were
similar enough.

Matching snow crystals
were discovered in
Wisconsin USA in 1988.

The crystals were not traditional
flakes but hollow hexagonal prisms
true moral of the snowflake story?

If you want to spend years
trying to identify
identical snowflakes in eye

matching detail; do not use error
random eye memory method
use instant point match computer.

Written in December 2010 on the 15.12.2010.

Faith Flights To
Flower Heavens

heart muscles surrounded in a reservoir of blood
pollen call is rainbow pot of gold to El Dorado
vessels of golden one flower air in fertilization
flights seed flowers in colours shapes miraculous

heavens ablaze with colour shape smell lure scent
heaven promise nectar pollen rewards await joy flight
heaven wing tips away thick bee hair pile insulation
heaven journey flights thick pile warm in cold weather

bumble bees fly flight build up electrostatic charge
flowers well grounded pollen lured electrostatically
attracted compelled to bumble bees pile when lands
pollen covered bee enter flower heaven charge pollen

pollen charged priority preferentially
attracted to stigma
stigma better grounded than other parts of visit flower
wealth amassed pollen all mother
load easy pick treasure
bumble bee pollination gifts life
to seed crops wildflowers

Written in October 2010 on the 30.10.2010.

52

Flights Of Impossibility

bumble bees fly upon wings impossible
black yellow fuzzy bodies heavy rise up
helicopters rise up hover off in buzz flight
bumble bees body mind looms large shiny

heavy thought cannot confined be earth bound
wings of hope lift weight impossible to soar
scientists proclaimed your flights impossible
faith was flight word transformative to bare load

Written in October 2010 on the 30.10.2010.

Pollen Call Is Rainbow Pot
Of Gold To El Dorado

walk within fields walk within woods
walk upon prairie grass or wild tundra
all is listening nature all nature listens
observe quiet hare sure big ears hears
but the bumblebee does not have ears
how then is it a fuzzy bumblebee hears

it is not known whether a bumblebee hears
it is not known how fuzzy bumblebee hears
a bumblebee could hear sound waves passing
sound waves soft passing through freedom air
a bumblebee can feel the vibrations of sounds
vibrations of sounds through wood materials

a bumblebee could hear sound through legs
a bumblebee could hear sound through fuzz
fuzzy body to kept warm to keep out winds
to keep out wind chill so as not to catch chills
a bumblebee watches golden pollen showers
a bumblebee dances among flowers for hours

pollen call is rainbow pot of gold to El Dorado
vessels of golden one flower air in fertilization
flights seed flowers in colours shapes miraculous
heavens ablaze seed colour shape smell lure scent
heaven kiss nectar pollen rewards await joy flight
flights of impossibility sow wild flower seed scent

Written in October 2010 on the 30.10.2010.

Out Gunned By A Single
Cell DNA Rocker

Amoebia Dubia approximately
200 times more DNA than a human
being of ego essential character.
Genome human 3.2 billion base pairs.
The largest sequenced genome known?
At present a one celled animal traveller.
Counting up in genome base pairs we have
E. coli 4.1 million, baker's yeast 12 million,
a worm 97 million, a fruit fly 120 million base pairs.

Continuing with our count up define
a flower arabidopsis *(Arabidopsis thaliana)* 157 million,
a bat *(Rhinolophus ferrumequinum)* 1.9 billion,
a snake *(Boa constrictor)* 2.1 billion
an Asian barking deer *(Muntiacus
muntjak vaginalis)* 2.5 billion
us humankind *(Homo sapien)* 3.2 billion
a frog (*Bufo bufo*) 6.9 billion
amoebia *(Amoeba proteus)* 290 billion
amoebia *(Amoeba dubia)* 670 billion base pairs.

Amoebia Dubia approximately
200 times more DNA than a human
when the human genome was
recorded as 2.9 million base pairs.

Human immunodeficiency
virus type, only 119,750 thousand?
A virus usually contains
less base pairs than a bacterium.

"Duplications are probably
fundamental to the creation
of genetic novelty."

"Horizontal gene transfer is a highly
significant phenomenon and amongst
single-celled organisms perhaps
the dominant form of genetic transfer."

"Horizontal gene transfer is invoked
to explain how there is often extreme
similarity between small portions
of the genomes of two organisms
that are otherwise very distantly related."

The words probably, perhaps and invoked
were used to indicate that we are not as knowledgeable
nor smart as collective public perceptions.

Artificial horizontal gene transfer
is a form of genetic engineering
which was once used for genetic warfare
biological weapons development

crossing the genetic barrier between
species to create a cold war advantage
such as the creation of the aids virus.

While the human race continues to deploy
scientific development to attain military supremacy
Amoebia Dubia continues rein supremacy
as the largest sequenced genome known to humanity.

Amoebia Dubia slam dunks the field and rocks on.

Written in December 2010 on the 27&29.12.2010.
Source of scientific data, "Sizing up genomes: Amoeba is king" by Edward
R. Winstead, February 12, 2001. Data updated by later source referenced.
Amoebia Dubia is still the largest, reference source
Parfrey, L.W.; Lahr, D.J.G.; Katz, L.A. (2008). "The
Dynamic Nature of Eukaryotic Genomes".

Life Principle

Everything that is
is inseparately alive.

All life
unique made manifest
is encoded
intricately interconnected.

All life is one life
all lusting to
live.

I communicate with
all existence I see
all life inherent
is not apart from me.

Creativity is
immaterial nature
made manifest
idealism more ennobled
than realized
contemporary reality.

An ecosystem
like planet earth evolving
is a closed system
vibrating indomitably aware.

Written in October 1999 on the 4.10.99.

Sacred Life Honoured

alternative lifestyles philosophies
retrieve perceive principle sacredness
of one life all life earth ecosystems

Written in November 1999 on the 12.11.1999.

The Common Sea
Of Humanity

'the sea so deep it never sleeps
by day or night it lives on . . . [perpetual] fight
against . . . [embattled] rocky coast
which is . . . [weathered worthy opponent] host

rushing ramming against . . .
[sea sculptured mountainside] . . .
[wave action causes whirlpool, boiling
swirling whirling, eddy rolling] quick fast dive

down below [flotsam surface]
its [more serene] calmer here
for no [crushing roaring] waves roll [disturbing
equilibrium as violently] way down here . . .'

Undercurrents are true demarcation lines
interactive beneath apparent surface of all things.

Surge tempest storm blasted vibrant sea,
so immensely powerful so immensely deep;
even in vortex hurricane force gale,
aquatic seascape to denizens lulls to sleep.

Wondrous sea home of seaborne eons
conceals creates multiple timeless mysteries
hidden by day by night through countless eternities.

The echo of something buried is
amplified in seashells roaring.
The echo of something buried is
drumming in cerebral inheritance.
The echo of something buried is shrouded
in serpentine chromosomes.

What forces in life savagely bark for separation?

Humanity is under an interdict to wander
as kernel Edenic sentence of declensions infused.
Endemic to pernicious nature.
Is healing quest for racial refuge.
A better world is shore. Whole shoal must swim for.

Written in May 1999 on the 19.5.1999.

A Golden Memory

When I was a young child
about five to seven years of age.
I noticed the neighbour's trees,
were dirty and sooty and black.
Black with smoke chimney coal dust.

The bark was ugly dirty and black
the leaves were ugly dirty and black.
And barely green if at all in most places,
except a little on the side facing the sun.
The sun I saw as a beautiful yellow light.

Next to my father's garage grew these trees,
they were really tall shrubs, but I was but still,
a young child; with much to learn in this world;
still ruled by men. Magic and the elfin language,
still danced like sparkling stardust in my eyes.

Next to my father's garage grew these trees.
They were so sad dull black lifeless and ugly.
I took a beautiful bright yellow lively house paint.
I painted the trees yellow bright golden yellow.
In all sad places I could short armed easily reach.

But I also got paint on my hands face clothes.
In my wonderful joy I got paint on my clothes.
My apparently best going to town best clothes.
My mother punished me for painting the trees.
All leaves a bright joyous happy yellow colour.

For painting making a small part
of this dull adult fading world.
A golden orb magical shinning
bright mystical fairy glade place.

> For trying to make the tired
> world a better magical place.
> Thus were childhood dreamers
> often beaten into submission.

> By those who failed to see
> the divine presence in dreams.
> By those who failed to see
> the magical sparkle in dreams.

Written in March 2000 on the 3.3.2000.

Burning Bright

These are
the last days
of the sun.

Behold the sun
is gloriously
burning bright.

The last days
of a solitary sun
burning into contemplation.

A bright supernova
among darker
background constellations.

I torched
am a stellar body
burning bright.

Come walk in
the consuming light
I leave for you.

I torched
am a stellar body
burning bright.

Come dance
come celebrate the passage
left by a blazing light.

Sun phoenix expanding
experientially exponentially
in ashen cosmic luminosity
momentary breath taking supernova.

Supreme beauty blazes forth
radiant seed of stellar soul.

Written in March 2000 on the 14.3.2000.

Let The Butterfly Fly Free

let the butterfly fly free spread her wings
upon a gentle wind while her wondrous wings
glitter in brilliant sunlight like an angel's wings
like tender heart of my love's sweet beating wings
her wondrous wings glitter through rainbow shades

Written in November 2000 on the 19.11.2000?

In Leaf Fall Learn

give leaf to leaven
busy hungry crawl caterpillar;
free to wander dawn
where it chance may

to spin silken
dream transition one glorious day;
to spin woven
dream seen inspiration as caterpillar

crawl in dust leaf learn
until time to metamorphosis turn;
dreams grounded stay
not earthbound stubborn

aspire to destiny blue cloud heaven
leap in faith learn to freedom fly;
patient be stretch birth beat wings dry
upon breath breeze sing embrace sky

Written in September 2010 on the 23.9.2010.

Metamorphosis

time melts
flux transitions

shadows
skin tissues

peeled minds
transmutations

Written in December 2010 on the 14.12.2010.

A Moment Of Clarity

Will Gift you
an insight into the world

Will Gift you
a reasoned reflective reality

Will give you a meditative poem
an insight into the meaning of shadows

glass perception is always
a kaleidoscopic view

object and interaction
the beholder and the beheld

a moment of clarity
between hastily filled spaces

Written in March 2006 on the 9.3.2006.

Wild Flower Leave For Future Contemplation

True artist encapsulate
wild exotic flower
lonely addicted traveler
so oft has sought.

To be found within distant
time chimed pilgrim journeys
in no famous city florist's
shop to be so easily bought.

Oh angry hand
would you rashly crush
an exquisite purchased
store bought flower?

Its petals one by one
to tear rashly apart
a petulant crime mystic
released scent may savour.

Leave growing free pluck
not solitary wild flower
alone it grows prolific
within rare sanctuary grove.

Another traveler one day
driven at appointed hour
savours delight an unlocked
flower enjoyed upon dusty drove.

Written in January 2010 on the 22.1.2010.

Embodied Transmutation

air breathed embodied
transmutes oxidizes grey clay
wild horses gallop across mind soul

Written in January 2010 on the 24.1.2010.

Embodied Transmutation Unleashed

breathed air embodied transmutes
oxidizes grey clay animated actions unleashed
wild horses gallop across soul mind

Written in January 2010 on the 24.1.2010.

Embodied Encapsulations

Life encapsulates transmutes
enslaves air breathed creatively . . .
transmutes oxidizes grey clay
particles dance Newton's waltz.

Who can stop tame wild horses
galloping within mind soul sung . . .
grey clay excited energized activated
string theory dances variant steps.

Hoof beats echo drum
infuse through fibres being.

Written in January 2010 on the 24.1.2010.

Koi

Chinese Carp swimming
in prestigious ornamental tank
prestige purchased expensively
for luck for tradition for prestige.

If you were ravenously hungry
would you eat lucky carp?
Would starving poor people
among you eat it gladly?

Written in January 2010 on the 24.1.2010.
Koi - a carp with red-gold or white coloring, kept as an
aquarium or ornamental pond fish. Native to: Japan, temperate
regions of East Asia. Latin name: Cyprinus carpio.

Event Horizon

escape darkness
black hole residue
remnant of fallen light

escape darkness
black hole residue
awesome all consuming density

walking edge
of event horizon
awaiting new entry point

come forth rebirth
entry into light
awaiting entry point resurrection

Written in January 2010 on the 27.1.2010.

Landscape Imagery

Nature was
and is still
the teacher
of poets who

strive words to get
landscape imagery,
moments glimpsed
in realism and sentiment

accurate the simple
elegance of snowflakes
is such a moment defined
a master of fallen restraint.

The woodlands
near my home
were as diverse
as native beech

with grey bark
deciduous leaves
or evergreens like
kauri and fern,

moss covered rocks,
perhaps it is time
to admit, nature and nature
poems are not for everyone.

Written in January 2010 on the 28.1.2010.

Snow And Rain

I have watched
and felt
both snow and rain
shaken

from bough
of tree limbs,
desired to linger
longer to watch

'Silent and soft and slow'
the first snow fall
as a new mantle
'Descends the snow'.

I wonder
if Longfellow
faced the same
dilemma,

the onset
of encroaching dark
or a possible
turn in the weather,

may necessitate
but the glimpse
with long hours
of hard hiking left

before
the days
journey
is over.

Written in January 2010 on the 28.1.2010.
Two quoted lines from "Snowflakes" by Henry Wadsworth Longfellow.

The Gift Of Art

The Camera
The Photographer
The Lighting
The Colour
The Pose

all serve you well . . .

this is indeed
an exceptional
photograph

a work of art
all can appreciate
all can admire

still yet I see
art all around me
art encompass me

the art of seeing
belongs
to the artist

eternally
expressed in art
eternally
defined anew

fleshed
out
in newly
evoked

forms
probing
boundaries
to be
transcended . . .

Written in February 2010 on the 1.2.2010.

An Inferno In Fuel
Passion Never Lit

rooftop fingerprints etch
into mind view over
horizons cityscapes entice

views all contrast weathers
wore in photographic lifetime
social flash freeze insights

rooftops never walked
upon in lives never
entered in languages

never spoken
in minds
never embraced

in souls shadows
seen intent
in shadows emotions

portraying status
to heightened enlivened
words spoken in

hearts eyes
flashing fires
of creative souls

split units
family units
educational units

potential enlightenment

pyramids are ultimate
rooftops on the world
apex to enter God states.

Written in December 2010 on the 19.12.2010.

Ancient Dust Of
My Homeland

Spirit of Mystic Aoteaora, enter into me
Land of Long White Cloud, enter into me
Spirit of My Forebears Ancestors, enter into me
Spirit you called Legendary Fairy Folk, enter into me

Spirit of ice capped southern mountains,
rivers forests glaciers, enter into me
Spirit of this old mystic majestic land,
encapsulating my birthright, enter into me

Dark majestic nights descend
upon wild west coast beaches,
Moonlight lapping serene wave tops
sparkling with ephemeral magic

Spirit of multitudinal diverse natures
Blowing in spray blown sea breezes,
Spirit of ancient dust of my homeland
Spirit of ancient Aotearoa, enter into me

Written in February 2010 on the 6.2.2010.
Aotearoa (pronounced [ao̯tea'roa]) is the most widely
known and accepted Māori name for New Zealand.

Dazzling Rift Valleys

original inspired canvas
not painted in splashed oils
etched in charcoal scratching
wind heat shimmers mirages

hot iron grains under bare foot
mica infused sparkling grey sands
waves of turbulent turning tide
surge in suck dazzling rift valleys

as salt chill water excavates myriads
of wind wave flowing leaping furrows
kaleidoscopic interchanges ephemeral
existence flows birthed deceased

across beachfront bay spanning
a single inlet among pristine variants
an entire shoreline of these isles enchanted
white surf rolls in awe inspiring

these are famed west coast beaches
heritage of my childhood kiwi homeland

Written in February 2010 on the 9.2.2010.

Torch Bearers

Are we not the torch bearers,
that uphold light in darkness,
that carry flames that burn,
from flickering time immortal,

we painted paintings upon cave walls
shaped sacred imaged life living,
upon three dimensional rock walls
within earth womb where life originates,

charcoal lines ochre invigorates life
dancing to light of ephemeral flames,
harmonics encaved resonant vibrations
tame visions within soul of earth mother,

power of our overlapping pictures imagery
flows throughout time throughout eternity,
symbolic outlines graphics images colours
pigment pipe airbrush blown across canvas,

interchanging interacting coupling bodies
permeate all aspects through porous time,
torched bodies dance, inspired ephemeral dances,
blazing torch light, burning mind to descent mind . . .

holder of spirits redeemable
throughout transcending ages,
holder of spirits entranced
attaining transcendental consciousness . . .

Written in February 2010 on the 11.2.2010.

Stir Like Flashes Of Moonlight

Memories of teenage summer nights
stir like flashes of moonlight
on North Beach sea waves at night

blurred water white crested sight
rolling in upon shadowed beach
next to Tip Head skimming illusions

polished images of how we were
seen through introspective lens
ghost cries of gull and youth

mingle then now through dimensions' change
some swam hard to catch wildfire lightning
to voice shock waves echo in new lands

Written in February 2010 on the 13.2.2010.

Children Of Dust

white man make
heap big smoke
but little light
no ancestral fire

white man steal
sacred thunder
make heap big

greed storms
blowing up sacred
swallowed world

white man
eats up earth
while dust
eats everything

choke dust
cover ground
blanket

white man
in earthen
burial cloth

so grass
may grow again
so river
may run again

so fish
may swim again
so buffalo
may swarm again

so great spirit
may seed renew life again
so earth mother
may bear in womb again

so red man
may worship creator again
worship great spirit
creator of heaven and earth

Written in February 2010 on the 16.2.2010.

Cultural Heritage Nurtured

quality not quantity
wisdom not trivia

take time
break
new ground

for planting

to plant
acorns
wisdom

budding
enlightenment

thriving into
generations
forthcoming

growing into
forest giant
kauri or

totara
varieties in
Aoteaora

water
seedlings
well

a great forest
is grown
over generations

centuries
millennia
life

is far
to short
to make

a joe
of
yourself

generations lost
are not soon
not easily recovered

Written in February 2010 on the 16.2.2010.
Aotearoa (pronounced [ao.tea'roa]) is the most widely
known and accepted Māori name for New Zealand.
Kauri an evergreen tree native to New Zealand. Latin
name: Agathis australis Totara Podocarpus totara (tōtara)
is a species of podocarp endemic to New Zealand.

Land Rape Earth Rape

Who cares what colour your skin
when you land rape earth rape
cut down pristine life giving forest
in the name of corporate profit
leaving but dust legacy mudslides.

Weep child the mighty totara is cut down fallen
no longer forests thick stretching 120 feet high
above dense canopy bird song broadleaf trees
linear sharp pointed leaves dark green-brownish
female totara flowers red swollen nut embedded.

Weep forests are ripped apart globally
who will purchase trees preserve forest
purchase inheritance diverse ecosystems
leave tress growing for children to explore
for friends descendants future generations?

Golden Totara your bark pattern is earth skin.

Written in November 2010 on the 29.11.2010.
Tōtara (podocarpus totara) is a beautiful tree endemic to New Zealand.

Transformation Peril

heart of many made poems
breathes among humankind
to be read at extreme risk of
transition transformation peril

Written in February 2010 on the 27.2.2010.

A Stone Griffin

a stone griffin
stern of heart
untouched
by exultant love

sits upon high
sits upon eves
in stone judgment
in heart of stone

face carved
in stone
emotionless
heartless

looking down
all passes
beneath sight
beneath grasp

look up
bodies inflamed
with emotions
passionate

we might miss
the light,
shining forth
from stars,

if we
do not,
raise
our heads,

to greater
expectations
emboldened
stellar blaze

Written in March 2010 on the 3.2010.

Drink Me Eat Me

the known world keeps
expanding contracting
with wondrous profusion

though potions drunk
wizard cakes eaten
are no longer necessary

when venturing through
kaleidoscopic looking glass
nor are rabbit holes needed

spy glass, magnifying glass, telescope,
microscope, radio telescope,
electron microscope, Hubble telescope,

amazing slices of perceived creation revealed,
expanding perceptions cosmic and microscopic
in a garden of rabbit hole worm hole replaced

an electron microscopic
images the sample surface
by scanning it with a high-
energy beam of electrons
in simple raster scan pattern

it's a kind of magic?
funny how we are never
far from the garden?

A raster scan, or raster scanning?

analogy; raster graphics, pattern image storage
transmission; used in computer bitmap image
systems; raster from Latin rastrum (a rake)
seek meaning; derived from radere (to scrape)

knowledge back in the garden rake over meaning?

rake earth over seeds
seeds of embryo ideas
fertile bed scatter ideas
choice seeds will grow

the pattern left by the tines of a rake,
when drawn straight, lines of a rake,
resembles parallel lines of a raster,
line-by-line scanning creates a raster

a systematic process of covering
an area progressively, one line at a time
is the rectangular pattern of image
capture and reconstruction in television

although a great deal faster
similar in most-general sense
to how one's gaze travels
when one reads text a poem

rastrum, an instrument
for drawing musical
staff lines, as we seek
celestial music universe
composed, in cosmic song

funny how
a Hubble telescope
with glasses
produced
ever more
detailed images

electron microscopy
a crystalline assembly
of electron diffraction
patterns of unstained

crystals show crystal
lattice sampling of
the coiled-coil molecular
transform to a resolution

beyond . . . a 'spot-scan'
method of electron imaging,
micrographs of unstained
crystals have been obtained

that visibly diffract laser
light from crystal spacings
as small as . . . a projection
map was calculated to . . .

using electron diffraction
amplitudes and phases
from computer-processed
images, the projection map

clearly shows modulations
in density arising from . . .
the first time this type of
modulation has been revealed?

truly we tumble ever further
down the rabbit hole
in quest controlled descent

crystals have *p*2 plane group
symmetry examinations of tilted
specimens shows the unit cell
only singular one molecule thick

possible modes of packing
of molecules in three
dimensions are discussed

eat me drink me
in ever smaller bigger
increments seems
we ever more must

Written in March 2010 on the 19&25.3.2010.

A Heritage Of Aussie Drought

Henry Lawson
was indeed a joy to read,
when studying Aussie lit,
he's so well writ

the rain is falling hard here,
season tropical Indonesian rain,
the scanned lines are fine
Lawson's writing succinct plain

Our Andy's gone to battle now
'Gainst Drought, the red marauder;'

but Australian Soil,
is still losing the battle,
to erosion drought
hard hoofed animals

like cattle sheep goats
horses donkeys pigs
but water buffalo camels?
and foxes cats rabbits?

over grazing combined
with cyclic natural drought
and feral invasive species
all have specific consequences

feral animals typically
have few natural predators
may carry fatal diseases
have high reproductive rates

a rabbit proof fence was
a kinda neat costly solution

i am no scientist but i'll tell you what i think

feral animals eat vegetation
which exposes fine soils
to wind and water erosion

cats kill birds, so what, you say?

cats destroy necessary birds
whose droppings carry seeds
seed grows renews vegetation

with less birds there is less vegetation
without vegetation the soil is exposed
to wind rain and hard hoofed erosion

raising salinity high water table still to beat
maybe satellite grazing is the answer sport?

drought still haunts Australia still,
but Andy's spirit was never beat,
now scientific Australia must beat,
the drought before its got us beat!

Written in January & April 2010 on the 27.1&16.4.2010.
This poem was written after reading the poem "Andy's Gone With
Cattle" by Henry Lawson, an Australian colonial writer and poet, who
is often referred to as Australia's greatest writer. Having taught causes of
Australian soil erosion, the temptation to mix the two was irresistible.

China Moon

Serene silent moon
draws out,
every possible
landscape,

every possible
culture,
as viewed
upon planetary plane,

calm imploring
untouchable,
mesmerizing
ancient universal pull,

twice-sized moon
is China Moon,
surreal to hunters
to legendary lovers.

Written in April 2010 on the 2.4.2010.

She Awaits A Moonlit Serenade

in the dark gentle stillness
in depths of night she waits for me
kind patient loving eternally

in soft warm tendril breezes
she waits for me night after night
she always comes eventually

in chill cold frost winter nights
still she comes by night she waits for me
in ghost lit pale serene beauty

in admiration admire her shape anew
this wonderful feeling experience share intensity
mystery passion is heartfelt endlessly

in nights constant enduring admiration
heart swells in appreciation together or alone
moon whispers sings vespers nocturnally

Written in October 2010 on the 23.10.2010.

Ego Of Immense Proportions

An ego
of stellar
proportions

has little
consideration
for a small

ice moon
orbiting
upon

the edge
of a far flung
solar system.

Written in April 2010 on the 11.4.2010.

Rhine Wine

our best times
are a fine wine
the mature wine

soil carefully tilled
years of planting
cultivating the vine

years of planting
growing pruning
fertilizing harvesting

harvest grapes
harvested aged
to be full drunk

by the firelight
in the evening
of our solitude

Written in April 2010 on the 12.4.2010.

A Second Sight

the day
daylight
is too dense
many minds

locked into
materialism
materialistic
concerns worries

material purposes
clay imprisonment
body form needs
demands dictates

sun bakes clay
cuneiform clay
tablets into rigid
fixed unbending

thought patterns
furnace hardened
in days progression
entrenched rigid set

the night
nightlight
night perceptions
night vibrations

soul released
aura vibrations
tune solar sail
celestial cosmic

interfacing energy
stellar wind transcribes
into thought flickering
images absorbing higher

dimensions focused
through inner knowing
third eye briefly seeing
written upon dark skies

aflame with star light
crossing stellar distances
carrying plasma light
code sentient deciphered

Written in May 2010 on the 11.5.2010.

Great Beauty Past And Present

Think of all the great beauty
still remaining in this world . . .
on land beaches rivers mountains

at sea beneath the ocean waves
all the species of incredible fishes
uncounted diverse marine life

in the air birds the fliers
insects in their myriads
bats gliders like squirrels

once flying also were pterosaurs
155 million years of powered flight
found on every continent except

Antarctica yet with over sixty genera
discoverd and flight skills equal
or exceeding birds (pterosaurs' had

massive flocculi, it occupied 7.5%
of total brain mass, far in excess of
all other vertebrate, birds flocculi 1

and 2% of total brain mass unusually
large flocculi; compared to other
animals, a science marvel, flocculus,

a brain region integrating signals
from skin, muscles, joints and
balance organs, sending out neural

signals to produce small, automatic
movements in eye muscles, to keep
the image on the pterosaurs' retina

steady; pterosaurs may have had
such a large flocculus because of
their large wing size, which would

mean that there was a great deal
more sensory information to
process) their preserved skeletons

must be fossilized in an iced Antarctica
that continent of huge undiscovered
fossilized marvels awaiting discovery

research new fossil discoveries paint
a fuller picture of an ancient lush past
secrets remain hidden in cold storage

98 percent of iced continent is covered
ice bound year-round by an ice layered
mass science will not penetrate probed

why laser tunneled depths publicly sealed
only a few islands along the Antarctic
Peninsula yield published finds recorded

authorities will tell you the first fossils
found were plesiosaurs marine reptiles
on Seymour Island in 1982; a hadrosaur

on James Ross Island in 1986, this first
dinosaur fossil, an ankylosaur, a duck-
billed dinosaur, first large plant eaters

found outside the Americas proving
proving; the continents past tropical
or temperate climate and vegetation

but what discoveries in Byrd Expedition?
(secret diary flights to land beyond poles)
on the sides of Mt. Weaver fossil plants

coal beds at South Pole within 200 miles
formed, by plants growing in profusion,
Ernest Shackleton reported coal proves;

past swampy areas, the growth of enough
plants, to produce an observed bed of coal
unknown wonders remain to be unearthed

Written in May 2010 on the 1.5.2010.

Hand Of The Infinite

aeons ephemeral beauty
balancing beautiful thought
contrast from gifted mind

to hand that gives bestows
images of an embellished infinite
sharing rare beauty perception

the hand of passion infinite
written into indelible patterned nature
written into seasons lessons

through years flows eternity
across life seasoned minds renewal
are sight sound felt senses

images spoken through whisper
whisper creation through eve receptive
serene cosmic harmony beautify

in spoken crystal moments
creation nature kaleidoscopic infuses
sparkles divinity personified

Written in June 2010 on the 4.6.2010.

Darkness Split Second Broken

Hot summer nights
still air no breeze
no sound yet all sound

universal cosmic sound
resounds through soul
heart of my inner being

playing tunes on threshold
below conscious thought
hearing acute soul perceives

energy pores drum beats vibrating
every atom of flesh quivers
fibres encompassing shell shape

ghost white full moon calls
to all earth children possessed
in receptive melody vision

light flashes upon retina
in darkness split second broken
while moon cloud swims

God takes another snapshot
for our album another flash
every decade captured thus

light plasma haunts moments
God delights in recording
a secret album awaiting soul

at end of destinies journey
soul charge flashes infused
battery powered up tasked

heavy drain usage awaits
predetermined inevitable
events in due series coming

inner purpose of life
discovered realized
listen to soul steps

authority to direct footsteps
was seed soul inscribed to
direct guide searchers feet

in called chosen moments
flashes infuse steal purpose
to awoken be in refinement

wrapped in veils darkness
night has always had too
much power to stir my soul

nature in cobweb moments
in startling scenes captures
imprints vision till needed

creator imprinted flash messages
mind prompts in creation to guide
receptive servants in journey home

Written in June 2010 on the 10.6.2010.

The Pelican Brief

a black page in journal of dire seas
fresh crude sludge landmine landmark
flowing oil seals fate of myriad lives

Written in June 2010 on the 25.6.2010.

The Pelican Brief:
Oil Sea Spoilt

fresh crude sludge landmine landmark lives
bloated blotted black page in journal of dire seas
flowing leaked oil seals fate of myriad species

Written in August 2016 on the 21.8.2016.

A River Dies

a river dies choked to gills
expiring upon industrial waste

sadly as the river dies the fish die drowned
oxygen starved exhausted extinguished

life was a web of light upon the water
life web torn broken discarded

water breathed life into river flowing
man breathed in death river choking

oxygen rich river was flush with fish
smell taste drink putrid pollution

Written in July 2010 on the 4.7.2010.

Unexpected Outcomes
In Transformation

realm earth or water
we may dive through water
physically penetrate

accept
in experience
in meditation

test embodied
in storm swim
or manipulate

as technological
control harnessed
exploited

abused
or converted
to new levels

of balance
or concepts
of usage

all of which
may have unexpected
outcomes in transformation

Written in December 2010 on the 6.12.2010.

Diamond Mine

earth salted in diamonds
is better than tears
for fame and for riches
many will dig deep
fabled treasures are lures
fools ever do seek

mining for precious hearts
carries through hard years
mining for precious true love
true wealth eventually it bears

Written in July 2010 on the 31.7.2010.

Photosynthesis Earth Sphere

All is changed now
once this island
was rich in nature's gift

streams rivers flowed clean to sea
many animals rich in freedom
lived roamed in woodlands jungle

pure spirits their minds walked
in life light shadows perception
each day joy in heat beats alive

to walk among nature in balance nurture
learn flora fauna species life cycles
keys to ecosystem harmonies interactive

balance in life energy sustains
renewable replaceable sustainable
harmonic perception maintains

viable life bubble photosynthesis earth sphere
rain forest violated raped deforested destroyed
when will governments learn to eat breathe ash?

Written in October 2010 on the 26.10.2010.

Into The Looking Glass

Who is viewer
of own reflected image?
Do you see en-fleshed
reality as youth,
radiant in bullet proof
life, embracing beauty,
or age en-fleshed;
as ancient life survivor?

Is held looking glass
in the hand of age or beauty?
Interesting is what each
woman sees, the now of youth,
or lined reality, of age
or memories of youth; that linger.
Some gaze deeply into
the glass, past surface experience.

Through the eyes of seeing
through eye of inner soul.

Does the young man see
in his face, reflection of girlfriend?
Is the sparkle in his eyes,
for her or the girl, he hopes to find?
Does he seek one or many?
The wild ones, are ever attractive.
Does the girl see the bride?
A man to be moulded into marriage?

Do people really desire
to see, themselves in the mirror?
Or do they look with hope
or dreams, fitting flesh accordingly?
Changing hair perfume clothes,
shape, is cosmetic transition.
Others re-sculpture entire body
to create, plastic fantastic.

Those who cannot stand reflection
find form, in hall of mirrors.

Reflections born of desire can be
mind interactive, blade dreams.
Some hate image bent through years
while others, embrace soul's journey.
Remember quote 'A monkey is superior
to man, in that when it looks in the mirror,
all it sees is a monkey.' Yet this is not true,
a monkey sees status and primacy paramount.

Each monkey sees, own others, integral place
interactive, dependent place; within the troop.

Written in July 2010 on the 25.7.2010.

Life Feasts Still Feed
Old Hunters

hunters' valleys hide among the hills
old hunters lived to time stay at home
beside warm fires at night age creeping
across limbs that strode mighty heights
muscles straining proud in stalking hunts

red deer dance years past venison gifts
grace upon tables receptive of bounty
memories of clean kills thrill old hearts
valleys holding life spirit beating free
valleys I no longer walk as I used to be

Written in August 2010 on the 26.8.2010.

Hidden Valley Within
The Bush

stepping into these lost ruins of gardens
a few fruit trees and flowers endure
where the old ghost homestead has fallen
lost in time decay life memories gone

who lived here where did their lives sped go
did their children move away to distant town
or city leaving this valley in serene dusk beauty
deer slip through bush to feed in still eternity

Written in August 2010 on the 26.8.2010.

Ghost Towns Up On The Hill

images remind of ghost towns left abandoned
few trees still fruit among ruins of yesterday
coal seams played out present miners live now
in towns scattered below now road connected

who wants to live in this mist in rain three thousand
feet and more up when the sea begs lapping far shore
upon this strip of coast a ribbon of blue beauty below
watch light dance upon the sea on sunny summer days

Written in August 2010 on the 26.8.2010.

Fruit Not Felled By The Wind

old fruit trees shedding petals in the wind
fragrant lily white petals strew green grass
before wedding of tree love born on wind
flowers endure grace old trees with fruit

Written in August 2010 on the 26.8.2010.

Beauty Is Found

On earth beauty is found in obvious
or sudden surprising hidden places
appreciate it all awesome wondrous
or delicate or incredibly small embraces

perfection is not for earth awaits in heaven

be glad for all grace all space all traces
of perfection each place of veneration

Written in September 2010 on the 19.9.2010.

Sun Seeking Flies

A crowd composed of sun seeking flies
now suns upon concrete door-step
sunning in light late afternoon sunshine

I wave my arms about them
they dance in late afternoon sunshine

I conduct a cloud of flies
in congruent rhapsody of aerial ballet

Written in May 1998 on the 2&3.5.98.

Fly Buzzing Naked Skin

The fly bothers me
with its buzzing,
its flight about upon

my naked
sun soaking up skin,
in this restorative moment

sustaining need
for unseasonably hot autumn,
sun soaking up relaxation.

Written in May 1998 on the 2&3.5.98.

Cloud Song

Clouds Beg Admiration
Ice Crystal Lattices
The Impossibility Of Identical Snowflakes
Sky Seeds Melting Snow
Watered Memories

Written in December 2010 on the 17.12.2010.

Ice Crystal Lattices

Snowflakes
frozen ice crystals
conglomerations

fall through
Earth
atmosphere

two snow
crystals
microscopic

supercooled
cloud
droplets freeze

variety
sizes
shapes

complex
shapes
emerging

as the flake
falls through
differing

temperature
humidity
regimes

individual
snowflakes
nearly

unique
in
structure.

Written in December 2010 on the 12.12.2010.

Clouds Beg Admiration

clouds wind race
over eternal skies
chasing dream horizons
whispering revelations

in hearts soul soaring
hearts touching sky
hearts swimming
cosmic wind surfing

solar winds waves
into universal mysteries
keys entice unlocking
moments in meditations

Written in December 2010 on the 17.12.2010.

An Indian Summer

alas sweet summer love
was but for a single season
an Indian Summer still can
be enjoyed without reason

some birds migrate in call autumn
to distant far foreign shores
some leaves fall in rainbow autumn
shedding to nature's firm laws

the treachery of heart kingdoms
flays us with cages of feelings
a heart seeking far freedoms
is not ours for sweet stealings

Written in August 2010 on the 30.8.2010.

An Eternal Summer

frozen chill landscape
sapping warmth lust rut life
leeching nutrients in brain
eating into marrow of bones

rivers streams lakes
entombed in ice age
continents stretch
weight white bound

too long too long perpetual winter ...
generations gone never ending ice...

birds migrate before chill winter sets in . . .
temporal species die hibernation appeals . . .

sleep on sleep on slumber in dormant stasis . . .
live off reserve body fat reduce pulse metabolism . . .

people also move to warmer or tropical climes
when cold and loneliness bite too deep
spring is a season of growing sap rising rebirth
birds fly follow the eternal summer sun

Written in September 2010 on the 24.9.2010.

Canvas Of Leaf Life Stories

restoration a kinda life season soul appeasement
light is still liquid paint shining upon autumn leaves
colours shapes shift blown across damp moss earth
tree roots snug cuddle warm under blankets of leaves

leaves to warm comfort sing mould harvest life stories
tell of spring quick at bud born to summer adventures
tell of bugs spirit climb ate birds leap skies flew sang ate
tell of glorious summer days star canvas summer nights

breeze prints encyclopedia comprehensive life whispers

Written in October 2010 on the 30.10.2010.

Serenade Under A Blood
Red Yellow Moon

even when all the art is burned and gone
alone high up in the raw Rocky Mountains
even in cold blues whites of bitter winter

lone wolf will serenade blood red yellow moon
alone in the night sitting serenades spectral moon
love serenade cry out to bewitching lover moon

sing in vast cathedral stellar unto the altar of light
sing in shadow horizons meteor burn in blazing light
sing in rhythms eternal to pulse rhythm moonbeat

lone silhouette in moonlight phantom of eternal night

Written in September 2010 on the 16.9.2010.

Transformation Seasonal
Or Life Shattering

transformation is manifest
seasonal or life shattering
but always life renewal seeks
the warmth of the earth
and bird flight of dreams

after darkness passes
comes new days
new experiences
and time which changes
all things in time streams

shaping creating diversity dissimilar
sow a poet engaging soul images
in spirit journeys of mind concepts
shift flow continue soul journey feel
the earth, air, wind, water, warmth, light
breaking through storm clouds fading

Written in December 2010 on the 6.12.2010.

I Saw The Lamp

Among gathering darkness
storm clouds brewing mists
still shines lamp light glow
welcome at street window

a welcome to warm cold heart
any passing stranger may enter freely
come embrace share this hearth
share meal break bread communally

come enter at the gate take off the shoe
each dipping bread into a dish of stew
true prophet prepared love meal to chew
false prophet preaches division to woe

affliction misfortune distress is a grief hate bred
woe betide a follower who regrets not all Dead
a message of love for your neighbour God Said
forgive leave revenge judgement to me God said.

Written in December 2010 on the 3.12.2010.

Life As Surface Realities

deeps depths of life
mystery
as deep
as the ocean

life as surface realities
far shores
waves which rock embraces
to reassure

to test
determination
of mind
liquid limbs

vessels
are often filled
with only that
which is sought

Written in December 2010 on the 6.12.2010.

Dominant Themes Flow
Through Life Lives

so many mist images
within dominant themes
flow through life lives

the flowing river
like liquid life
with horizons
diverse distant

mystical
geometrical
merging
horizon sky

time splices
perceptions
destinations
value sticks

Written in December 2010 on the 6.12.2010.

Life Time Transformations

so many mist images
within dominant themes
flow through life lives

the flowing river
like liquid life
with horizons
diverse distant

mystical
geometrical
merging
horizon sky

deeps depths of life
mystery mysteries
as deep as oceans
life as surface realities

far shores
waves
traverse oceans
which rocks

embrace to reassure
test determination
mind muscled limbs
depart upon journeys

vessels
are often filled
with only that
which is sought

measure realm
earth or water
we may dive through
water physically

accept in experience
accept as meditation
test embodied
in storm swim

or manipulate
as technological
control
harnessed

exploited
abused
or converted
to new

levels of balance
or concepts of usage
all of which may
have unexpected outcomes

in transformation
transformation is manifest
seasonal
or life shattering

but
transformation
always
life renewal seeks

the warmth
of earth
bird flight
dreams

after darkness
passes
comes
new days

new experiences
and time
which changes
all things

but in time
streams
diversity
dissimilar

sow a poet
engaging
soul images
in spirit journeys

mind concepts
continue
the journey
feel

the earth
air wind
water
warmth

light
light breaking
through storm
clouds fading

Written in December 2010 on the 6.12.2010.

Earth Pulse

ash
dirt
dust
solid
earth
ground
terra firma
solidity stasis
earth murmur
heart murmur
shock earthquake
sudden heart attack
life pulse curve quirk
shake up tremor killers
aftermath scenes surreal
distorts harmonic flow
after shocks rhythmic
raw heart beat surge
cost displacement
miss monuments
rock time counts
fallen edifices
bodies rigid
shattered
seismic
ground
waves
flow

Written in October 2010 on the 6.10.2010.

Angels Harmonic Serenade

stand upon thrilling flame sunlight lit cliff
above vast stretching river carved canyon
heights determination siren embryo calling

run fast take swift leap embracing wings faith
launch into flowing solar wind ride cosmic void
solar flares rapture songs of mind soul soaring

beams radiant pulse divine plasma joy of flight
angels harmonic serenade new birth form spreading
infinite light transcends vibrant flesh transforming

Written in August 2010 on the 28.8.2010.

Stardust Seeds Dream Life

sprinkled star dust
falls descends upon
a troubled life earth

stardust is not wasted
where fallen upon water
stardust seeds dreamlife

gift of embryonic oceans
stardust seeds leap land life
star gazing distance heavens

wolves sing to silver moon
soul serenade glow stars
moths flutter dance starlit

webs shining perceived
in strung earth sphere
fly star beams solar seed

creation spell cast dreams
stardust fills eyes souls
in star gazers vision seeded

writing silent love notes
sparkling pedestal beautified
solar divo earth heartthrob

necklaces diamond glass
set in stillness echoes
singing prima dona solo

light lit symphony
dream celebration
opera tribute eternity

Written in October 2010 on the 9.10.2010.

A View Through
Depths Of Creation

stars twinkling in orchestra
of canopy cosmic night skies
light piercing cosmic void
as arrows lit shot across compass
light echoes back light years
100,000 years a galaxy across
spun with wonder twinkling
folding back creative histories

planets circling around perceived
stars science proves abound
life upon planets in votive
harmony sings to creator profound
universal whole expands
upon love design creator's choice
glowing growing star splendors
strike filament eyes receive rejoice

a journey of mind cosmic proportions
a journey through into depths of creation.

Written in August 2010 on the 18.8.2010.

Love Cast In Spotlight Eternity

Love has had a cast
of millions millions billions
throughout history . . .

but it is always
the personification
of a single dancing . . .
or kissing couple.

It is the essential
single solitary pair
standing glowing . . .
in the spotlight of eternity.

Written in March 2000 on the 11.3.2000.

Dreams Rise Up

dreams rise up
in soft glows
aspiring heaven
lit perfection

the lover of dreams
took twelve hundred
slip coloured balloons
with care blew each up

to release these mind
singing symbols mind
stirring free to rise up
into awaiting air then

for the eternal beauty
of dark velvet starlit
night released twelve
hundred lit warm glowing

lanterns to complement
God's glory created
in a universe of light
complete perfect unity

the lover of dreams
smiled as each soft
spoken dream departed
in love in mind flight

to places unseen
in depths of hazel
dove eyes love relit
in wonder glowing

in sparkle soft glow
as stars sky danced
with flame lanterns
in a glorious soul

sight inspiring dreams
God above smiled in
gift human appreciative
dreams while angels

creation wide sang
tribute to our heavenly
creator time passed
in life times spent in

a love of inspiring
dreams till eyes still
aglow did finally close
on life earthly dreams

then to maestro composer
of all creation wondrous
alive soul departed in loves
worship embracing divine God

with new soul born heavenly
dreams in immaculate eyes
a precious red-coloured jasper
stone glows rainbow emerald

Written in December 2010 on the 8.12.2010.

Let Me Arise To Sigh Over

let me arise to sigh over, shining every gift morning,
let me arise to sigh over, glorious every breath day;

celebrate soft sighs of love, ever sighing ever missing,
moments due longing, in desire
to return to, our beloved;

soul sings song of life renewal, love
weaves new strands life,
walk in paradise at water's edge,
braided love walks into night.

Written in July & December 2010 on the 4.7.2010 &14.12.2010.

'Still I Rise' by Maya Angelou Do You?

Indomitable will of humanity
to rise from oppression
slavery all odds uncounted

the will of those who cannot
bend the knee to ultimately
triumph over injustice adversity

Maya Angelou claims birthright
to rise through history rise rise
rise to aspired to promised land.

Written in August 2010 on the 15.8.2010.

www.ingramcontent.com/pod-product-compliance
Lightning Source LLC
Chambersburg PA
CBHW030445290526
45786CB00001B/458